MONSTER KNOWS I'M SORRY

by Connie Colwell Miller

illustrated by Maira Chiodi

PICTURE WINDOW BOOKS
a capstone imprint

At Plooble School, it's time to learn!

Let's work! Let's play! Let's do!

ABC

3-1=2

a

THANK! you!

I'm Sorry!

2

Monsters work on math and words,
and learn their manners too.

Hello!

Love

$\begin{array}{r} 3 \\ \times\ 4 \\ \hline 12 \end{array}$

PLEASE!

Ii

5+3=8

At school the monsters rush about
to put away their things.
"I'M SORRY, friends. I can't talk now!
School starts when that bell rings."

5

The monsters all sit at their desks
to start the school day strong.

One monster isn't listening.

Another monster in the room
looks like she is sad.

Monster puts an arm around her.
"I'M SORRY you feel bad."

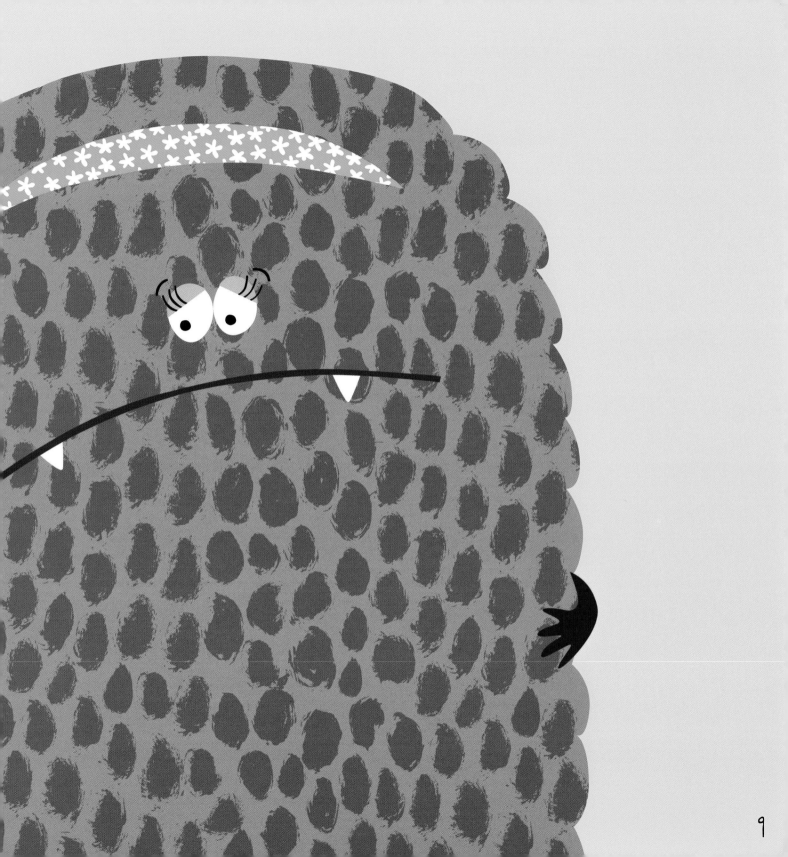

During free time all monsters play
a game of Zip and Boing.

A monster is left out somehow.
"I'M SORRY. Care to join?"

13

It's time for snacks—splurg and dee.

"Oh, no! There's no more dee!"

Monster says, "I'M SORRY, friend.
Want to share with me?"

15

At sharing time one monster frowned.

She didn't want to share.

She hid her toy from her friend.

I'M SORRY. THAT WASN'T FAIR.

17

Art class now. But a monster spills.
There's floogle on the floor.

"I'm really very SORRY, friends.
I hope that there is more!"

19

Teacher says, "It's story time."

One monster says, "No way!"

Soon he feels awfully bad.

"I'M SORRY. I like to play."

PLOOBLE SCHOOL

I'M SORRY we must go, my friends.
The school day is done.

We're off to walk back home now.
But we all had so much fun!

23

READ MORE

Bently, Peter. *Say Please, Little Bear.* New York: Sandy Creek, 2011.

Dahl, Michael. *Mouse Says Sorry.* Hello Genius. Mankato, Minn.: Picture Window Books, 2012.

Mulcahy, William. *Zach Apologizes.* Minneapolis: Free Spirit Pub., 2012.

INTERNET SITES

FactHound offers a safe, fun way to find Internet sites related to this book. All of the sites on FactHound have been researched by our staff.

Here's all you do:

Visit *www.facthound.com*

Type in this code: 9781479522019

Super-cool stuff!

Check out projects, games and lots more at
www.capstonekids.com

Look for all the books in the series:

Thanks to our adviser for his expertise, research, and advice:
Terry Flaherty, PhD, Professor of English
Minnesota State University, Mankato

Editor: Shelly Lyons
Designer: Ashlee Suker
Art Director: Nathan Gassman
Production Specialist: Laura Manthe
The illustrations in this book were created digitally.

Picture Window Books are published by Capstone,
1710 Roe Crest Drive, North Mankato, Minnesota 56003
www.capstonepub.com

Library of Congress Cataloging-in-Publication Data
Cataloging-in-publication information is on file with the Library of Congress.
978-1-4795-2201-9 (library binding)
978-1-4795-2964-3 (board book)
978-1-4795-2952-0 (paperback)
978-1-4795-3327-5 (eBook pdf)
Written by Connie Colwell Miller

Printed in the United States of America in North Mankato, Minnesota.
092013   007772CGS14